# DIRTY AND DANGEROUS JOBS

# Pest Control Worker

DISCARD

## By Jessica Cohn

**Reading Consultant:** Susan Nations, M.Ed.,
Author/Literacy Coach/Consultant in Literacy Development

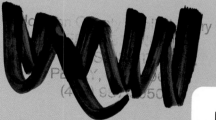

**Marshall Cavendish**
Benchmark
New York

Published by Marshall Cavendish Benchmark
An imprint of Marshall Cavendish Corporation

This publication represents the opinions and views of the author based on the author's personal experience,
knowledge, and research. The information in this book serves as a general guide only. The author and
publisher have used their best efforts in preparing this book and disclaim liability rising directly and
indirectly from the use and application of this book.

Other Marshall Cavendish Offices:
Marshall Cavendish International (Asia) Private Limited, 1 New Industrial Road, Singapore 536196 •
Marshall Cavendish International (Thailand) Co Ltd. 253 Asoke, 12th Flr, Sukhumvit 21 Road,
Klongtoey Nua, Wattana, Bangkok 10110, Thailand • Marshall Cavendish (Malaysia) Sdn Bhd,
Times Subang, Lot 46, Subang Hi-Tech Industrial Park, Batu Tiga, 40000 Shah Alam, Selangor
Darul Ehsan, Malaysia

Marshall Cavendish is a trademark of Times Publishing Limited

All websites were available and accurate when this book was sent to press.

Library of Congress Cataloging-in-Publication Data
    Cohn, Jessica.
       Pest control worker / by Jessica Cohn.
    p. cm. — (Dirty and dangerous jobs)
    Includes index.
    ISBN 978-1-60870-176-6
    1. Pest control industry—Employees--Juvenile literature. 2. Pests—Control—Juvenile literature.
    3. Hazardous occupations—Juvenile literature. I. Title.
  HD9718.5.P472C64 2011
  623.9'6023—dc22
                                          2010000208

Developed for Marshall Cavendish Benchmark by RJF Publishing LLC (www.RJFpublishing.com)
Editor: Richard Hantula
Design: Westgraphix LLC/Tammy West
Photo Research: Edward A. Thomas
Map Illustrator: Stefan Chabluk
Index: Nila Glikin

**Cover:** A worker sprays a huge wasps' nest in the attic of a house.

The photographs in this book are used by permission and through the courtesy of: Cover: Simon
Battensby/Photographer's Choice/Getty Images; 4, 7, 8, 15, 17, 19, 20, 22, 27: iStockphoto; 6: ROLAND
WEIHRAUCH/dpa/Landov; 7: © Arco Images GmbH/Alamy; 9: Scott Bauer/USDA; 11: Kage Manfred P/
OSF/Photolibrary; 13: © Elspeth Graham/Alamy; 16: © age fotostock/SuperStock; 21: Courtesy National
Library of Medicine; 24: Getty Images; 25: © Paul Glendell/Alamy; 28: AP Images.

Printed in Malaysia (T).
135642

# CONTENTS

Words defined in the glossary are in **bold** type
the first time they appear in the text.

Ants are common pests in many areas.

On the screen, a man is standing in a doorway leading into a room. He wears a simple uniform. He is surrounded by shadows. He is carrying a weapon. The man looks left and right. The man seems to be trying to hear and see a hidden enemy.

The room is dark. It is hard to tell how large the space is. The man listens to what sound like small **creatures** moving fast on the floor. They are squeaking, and there seem to be many of them. The man moves carefully into the room.

Suddenly, an angry buzz is heard. It grows louder. The screen fills with insects that look like monsters. There is a storm of beating wings. Long yellow teeth flash!

A video game player starts to press buttons: *Click! Click! Click!* The player battles the creatures. Then, suddenly, the screen flashes, "Game over!"

## Real Pests

In the world of video games, a player may battle creatures such as monster insects or giant rats. Knocking out a creature might earn the player points. But if the player makes the wrong choices, the game may be over. It may also end if the player moves too slowly.

In the real world, pest control workers battle live creatures. Their job is to keep people safe from pests such as bugs and rats. It takes them into places that may be hard to reach. In these places, it may be hard to see. To do their job, pest control workers sometimes have to check dark rooms. They shine lights into attics and basements. These places sometimes hold surprises.

The places where pest control workers go can also be risky. Their work takes them into dirty spaces under houses and onto the roofs of buildings. They sometimes enter dangerous buildings that are ready to fall down. Pest

### Attic Surprise

Jim Rutherford owns a pest control company in Michigan. He once found a big beehive in a dark attic. The bees' nest was eight feet (2.4 meters) high, and just as wide. "When you stood next to it," he says, "it sounded like a transformer"—an electric-power device known for the buzzing noise it makes.

A worker tries to kill insects that have made a nest under the roof of this building.

control workers need to be careful. If they make wrong choices, they risk getting hurt or catching a disease.

## Pest Problems

The pests that workers hunt down are creatures that bother people or creatures that harm people or property.

The problem can be small, such as ants on a deck. Or it can be major. Certain kinds of pests can destroy crops. Some pests, such as carpenter ants, can eat through the walls of homes and businesses. They cause damage that costs people a lot of money.

Even worse is the risk of disease. Rats and roaches are common after natural disasters such as strong storms. They can carry deadly diseases. When Hurricane Katrina caused

Rats may carry diseases.

flooding in New Orleans in 2005, dirty water filled the city. As the water went down, the number of pests went way up.

## Animal Invasions

All creatures have a natural **habitat**—the surroundings in which they normally live. Animals may become pests when they move into areas where they are not welcome. Sometimes, pests are animals such as bats, birds, or even deer. Often, pests are insects. People may put up with a

Bees are useful insects, but they can also be pests.

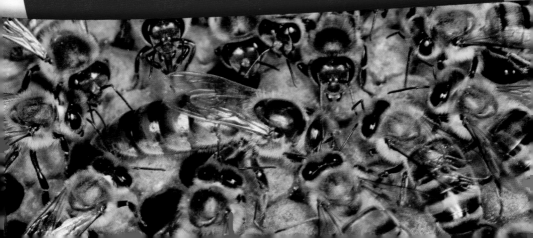

# The Most *Unwanted* Pests

According to the National Pest Management Association, a group devoted to pest control work, these pests are among the ones people are most likely to call pest control workers about:

- **Rodents:** Mice and rats damage property and spread disease.
- **Roaches:** Dust from cockroaches and their droppings can cause problems for people with an **allergy** to roaches. If the dust enters the air, persons with the condition known as asthma may find it hard to breathe.
- **Termites:** These insects eat wood and other materials and can cause costly harm to property.
- **Spiders and ticks:** These biting bugs, unlike insects, usually have eight legs. (Insects have six legs.)
- **Biting insects:** Biting insects such as mosquitoes have been blamed for spreading many sicknesses. Bedbugs are not known to spread disease, but their bites can be painful.
- **Stinging insects:** Some people get sick if stung by bees and wasps.
- **Ants and pantry pests:** People want to keep their food safe from bugs.
- **Wildlife:** When birds or other animals, such as raccoons or deer, get into people's homes, the result can be trouble.

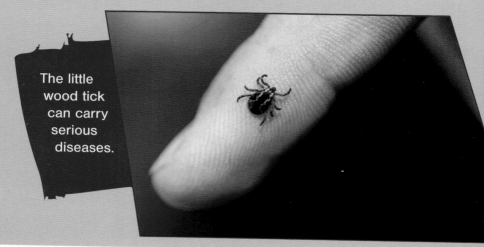

The little wood tick can carry serious diseases.

few ants at a picnic. But ants in a hospital are pests. Bees are important insects. They help flowers grow, and they are the source of honey. But bees that fly into a person's home are pests.

Pest control workers are called into action when pests cause damage, discomfort, or disease. Often by the time the workers are called, the pest problem is already serious, making the workers' job dirty and dangerous.

## Armed for Battle

Pest control workers have many different tools they can use. They may lay traps to catch mice, squirrels, and other animals. They may spray chemicals called **pesticides**. Some of these chemicals are used to drive pests away. Others are poisons that kill pests. Workers also use **bait** containing food. Pests come to get the food. The bait may be connected with a trap for catching the pests, or else it may contain poison that can kill the pests.

There is more to a pest control worker's job than just catching or killing pests. The job also involves checking to

This bait contains a chemical that kills cockroaches.

make sure the pest problem is really solved. For example, mice may enter a home during the winter, to get warm. A worker may get rid of the mice. There may be no sign of the creatures during the following summer. But when winter returns, mice start showing up again. It's possible that the first mice left "calling cards." Perhaps they dug holes in a corner of the house. They may have left traces that other mice could follow. A good pest control worker can help the people in the house think about ways to deal with such problems.

Pest control tools include baits, traps, and poisons. But the best tool that pest control workers have is their knowledge. They go to classes to learn about the pests they fight.

Skilled workers know the habits of the pests. They know where and how the animals tend to eat. Armed with all this knowledge, they can best decide what to do and what not to do. Suppose, for instance, the problem is moths, which eat clothing. "You need to know what time of year they lay their eggs or when they [lose their wings]," says Rutherford. "If you don't, you can do the wrong things."

## Sniffing Out the Problem

If one method of controlling pests can't do the job, pest controllers may find another that can. That is what they have done with an insect called the tomato pinworm. This bug kills tomatoes. Using pesticides to control pinworms doesn't always work well. The worms may just dig deeper into the tomatoes.

Luckily, there's another approach to the problem. Pest controllers can use special chemicals called **pheromones**. Many kinds of animals make pheromones. These chemicals

## Waking Up to Bedbugs

Bedbugs come out at night to feed on the blood of warm animals. These bugs are happy to feed on animals in a barn. But they will feed on sleeping people, too, if given the chance.

Long ago, bedbugs were a problem in the United States. Around the middle of the twentieth century, pesticides like DDT began to be used. These were very good at killing the creatures. As a result, bedbugs became rather rare. The only time many people heard about them was in the children's rhyme "Good night, sleep tight / Don't let the bedbugs bite." But then it became clear that DDT could hurt not just the pests but also other animals, and people as well. Its use as a pesticide was made illegal. In time, the insects began to spread. Now bedbugs are again a problem in some parts of the United States.

Tiny bedbugs can look scary when seen close up.

often take the form of smells. When an animal gives out a pheromone, other animals of the same type will recognize the pheromone and react to it in some way.

Pest control workers use the pinworms' pheromones against the bugs. They put tubes of pinworm pheromones around tomato plants. The smell from the tubes confuses the worms. It keeps the worms from finding each other. As a result, they cannot reproduce. This approach works without hurting the tomatoes. It also causes no danger to people.

## Pest Detectives

To do their job, pest control workers have to be detectives. They try to find the answers to key questions about the pests that they have to control. They ask questions such as "How did the pests enter?" and "What brought them here?" Knowing the answers can help solve the problem. Depending on the type of pests, workers may try to kill them or scare them away. Sometimes they will make sure an area is cleaned in a special way.

Finding the answers to the questions is not always easy. In 2009, bedbugs took over parts of a United Nations (UN) building in New York City. The building had no beds, so this was a surprise. One idea was that the bugs had entered the building on blankets and other items used by a moving company. Movers had recently carried items into the building. No matter how the bugs got into the building, they had to be killed. The UN has a lot of papers, and there were worries that the pests would hide in the papers. To get rid of the bugs, workers went in and sprayed poisons. To make sure the pests were gone, the workers then went through with dogs trained to smell bedbugs.

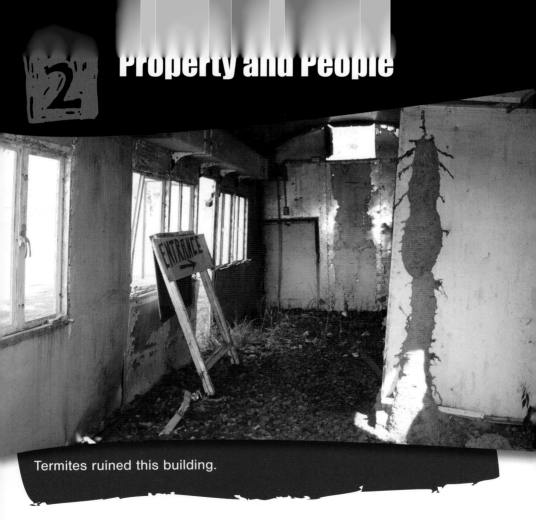

Termites ruined this building.

Armies of insects live in the ground. Among them are termites. These insects usually live in large underground colonies, but they come up to feed. They are very fond of eating wood. They will eat trees and bushes, but they like to dine on wood in buildings, too. As termites eat through a house, they leave hollow places in the wood. They may put dirt and mud in the hollows. Over time, the wood falls apart. Each year, termites cause billions of dollars in damage to trees and to houses and other buildings in the United States.

Like many other pests, termites are usually good at hiding. But young termites sometimes act in ways that give away the colony's presence. When the weather warms up or is rainy, young termites with wings come out. They fall to the ground and lose their wings. Then they look for a mate. Seeing these pests near a building is a clue to get help. Getting rid of termites is a task most people cannot do on their own. They need to call a **professional**.

## Silent Treatment

Pest control workers are trained to know where and why termites enter buildings. Termite paths are usually hidden, but a worker checks the whole building, looking for clues. Tubes of mud are one sign of the presence of termites. These tubes are tunnels that the insects build. Termites use the tunnels to go back and forth from the building to the ground. "They are built of [spit] and waste matter and dirt," says Michigan pest control expert Jim Rutherford. Most of the time, the tunnels are as thick as a pencil and run up and down a wall. But Rutherford has also seen larger tunnels, like those that children build at a beach.

Pesticides can be used on termites as they journey between the building and their home in the ground. One type of pesticide repels, or drives away, the termites.

### Taking the Bait

Sometimes modern technology can be a big help in controlling termites. One of the newer control methods uses special bait stations. These stations—the containers holding the bait—are equipped with a tiny **microchip**. The microchip can send signals. If termites show up at the station, the microchip sends a message that can be detected by pest control workers. In this way, workers can know when termites are on the scene.

The mud tube along this wall was made by termites.

A second type kills them on the spot. There also are pesticides that can kill the insects later. Such slow-acting poison may be put in baits made of paper or cardboard, which termites eat.

Getting to the termites can be hard, depending on how the building is constructed. Workers sometimes use drills that cut through concrete. They build tunnels for the poison. Then they pump in poison from tanks. Some of the tanks are small enough to roll or carry to the building. Others are attached to the backs of trucks.

## Danger in the Air

Pesticides strong enough to kill termites may also be bad for people. Some pesticides have been blamed for diseases that affect the way people move. Certain types of cancer seem to be linked to the poisons, too. Pesticide containers carry an important label. It describes the dangers involved in using the pesticide, and it notes safety measures that should be taken.

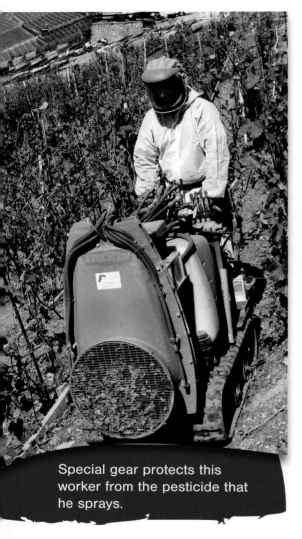

Special gear protects this worker from the pesticide that he sprays.

"All pesticides are dangerous," says Richard Fagerlund. He is known as "The Bugman." He has been working in pest control for nearly 40 years, and he writes about pest control for a newspaper in San Francisco. "The workers should wear the protective gear [talked about] on the label," he says.

Pest control workers usually wear gloves and clothing that cover their skin. If the pesticide is a spray or a dust that can get in the air, workers may need to put on special breathing masks called **respirators** so they do not breathe the poison or get it in their eyes.

It is especially important to keep children away from pesticide, and workers take special steps to keep children safe. Since children are smaller than adults, they can be more easily affected by even a small amount of poison. The brains of small children are not done growing yet, and they may be easily damaged. It is also important to keep pets away from pesticide. Pets are often curious. They do not know they should leave the poison alone.

## Danger and Discomfort

Another on-the-job danger is the possibility of being attacked by pests. Pest control workers have been bitten and stung. When Rutherford found the giant beehive, it

### Strong Poison

A pesticide is a product made to kill or chase off plants or animals that are pests. Certain cleaning products also kill some pests, but pesticides are different. Pesticides contain a stronger poison.

The Environmental Protection Agency (EPA) is the chief government agency overseeing pesticides in the United States. It divides pesticides into two main kinds: "general use" and "restricted use." General use pesticides are not considered very dangerous. Restricted use pesticides are quite poisonous. The EPA has rules for how those pesticides can be used and who can handle them.

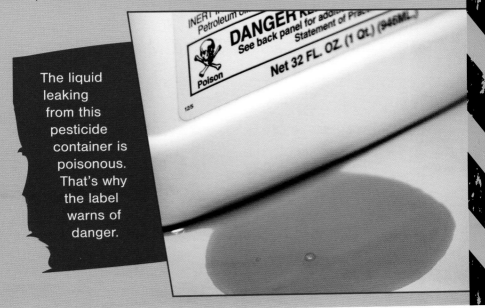

The liquid leaking from this pesticide container is poisonous. That's why the label warns of danger.

certainly got his attention. He has an allergy to bees. Some people who are allergic to bees have died from bee stings. To avoid being stung, Rutherford wore a protective bee suit, including gloves.

The work also can be simply uncomfortable. Pest control is carried out both indoors and outdoors. Work must be done in high heat and in the cold. Because pests like to hide, workers often have to go into uncomfortable spots. They move on their bellies under houses. They bend under roofs. They go up high ladders to reach nests above ground.

The work also can be uncomfortable in other ways. When a building has pests, the people there are often afraid or ashamed. They worry that others will think they are dirty. As a result, they may not be totally cooperative with pest control workers.

Pest control workers deal with dirt and danger. But the job is fulfilling for the workers who do it right. Pest control workers figure out problems and fix them. They help people live a more pleasant life. Because pests can cause disease, controlling them lets people live longer.

## Fully Outfitted

Making pest control equipment is a big business. A variety of tools and machines are produced. There are special lawn trucks with side windows that open in many directions. The trucks come with pumps and engines. Sprayers are often made with long hoses that roll up in the backs of trucks. Other sprayers can be carried like luggage. There are foam machines that look like a cross between a vacuum, a lawn mower, and a golf cart.

Among the smaller tools are those that test how much water is in the air or dirt. There even are tools to help workers fix bait stations that break.

# New Challenges

Standing water makes a good breeding place for mosquitoes.

Pest control workers hunt pests in crowded cities, where disease can spread fast. They control pests in rural areas, keeping the food supply safe. They commonly work in homes, at businesses, or on farms. But sometimes they take part in larger efforts, such as mosquito **abatement** programs. To abate something is to reduce it. In some cases, reducing mosquitoes can protect people's health.

Mosquitoes can carry diseases. For example, some mosquitoes carry a tiny life-form known as the West Nile **virus**. This virus most often is found in birds. Mosquitoes that bite sick birds can carry the virus to other living things. Most people who get the virus do not feel sick. About 20 percent of people have mild problems after catching it.

**MOSQUITO ALERT**
MOSQUITOES ARE
PRESENT IN THE AREA
FOR YOUR SAFETY
WEAR LONG SLEEVES
AND LONG PANTS
USE PROPER INSECT
REPELLENT
TAKE EXTRA
PRECAUTIONS AT
DUSK AND DAWN

Signs like this remind people to protect themselves against mosquitoes, which may carry disease.

They might have fever or might get a rash. Their body might hurt. Sometimes they feel a sore throat or pain below the stomach. But about 1 in every 150 people gets a serious form of the disease. It has been deadly in some cases.

## Coordinated Efforts

No medicine cures disease caused by the West Nile virus. So it makes sense to avoid the problem from the start. Government agencies provide advice on ways to avoid being bitten by mosquitoes. They tell people to use insect repellent and to wear long pants and sleeves at dusk and dawn. That is when mosquitoes are most active. People

### Picture of Health

West Nile virus was first found in the African country of Uganda in 1937. The virus first showed up in Europe in the 1960s. It appeared in the United States in 1999. In North America people get the disease mainly in summer and early fall, when mosquitoes are more active. Some years, there are more cases than others. California, for instance, had 880 cases in 2005. Nineteen people died. The next year, there were just 278 cases and 7 deaths.

## Trading One Problem for Another

Pest control workers have to be careful not to solve a pest problem in a way that creates a more serious problem. Sometimes, killing may not be the best way to deal with pests.

Years ago, Mao Zedong was the leader of the People's Republic of China. He declared that four pests needed to be killed: rats, flies, mosquitoes, and sparrows. Why sparrows? The birds were eating the seed from which grain grew. So the people tore down nests. They banged on pots to scare the birds away. The bird population went down.

This led to a new problem, however. The population of the insects known as locusts went up. The sparrows had been eating the insects. When the birds were killed, the locusts took over. They ate a lot of the crops. China also had other problems around that same time. For example, there was very little rain. The lack of rain meant that few crops grew. The locusts made the situation even worse. There was not enough food to go around. About 30 million people died of hunger.

This 1964 poster calls on the Chinese people to fight four pests: rats, flies, mosquitoes, and sparrows.

are also told to empty water from containers, such as flowerpots and barrels, because mosquitoes leave eggs in standing water.

In addition to giving advice, government agencies take steps to kill mosquitoes in areas where the virus has shown up. Often they learn about the presence of the virus by testing dead birds. If a bird is found to have the

Airplanes are used to spray pesticide over large areas.

virus, the area can be sprayed with pesticide. Some experts recommend spraying as far as 2 miles (3.2 kilometers) from where a diseased bird is found. Pest control workers do the spraying from airplanes or from moving trucks.

## Global Swarming?

For pest control workers, new challenges keep showing up. People have always been bitten by mosquitoes. But conditions affecting all living things, including pests, are changing. The temperature at the surface of Earth is higher, on average, than it was 100 years ago. This warming has affected pest activity. During warm winters and early springs, insects and other animals are especially active. Pests such as mosquitoes have become more active. Pests that kill crops have reached new areas.

## Other Factors at Work

Change in weather is not the only cause of new challenges. Even things such as new laws can create new problems. So may changes in people's travel habits. What happened with

## Red Fire Ants

One of the best-known pests to come to the United States from another country is a reddish type of fire ant. Fire ants are known for their ability to sting. The sting of the type from abroad is especially painful. This type originally lived in South America. It got into the United States in the 1930s. Scientists think the ants came on ships. The ants, often called red imported fire ants, are today found in many states of the South. They usually live in large groups below the ground.

The ants go after anyone who bothers them. They sting at least 5 million Americans every year. About 2 percent of these people need medical help. One percent of the people stung are allergic and in the greatest danger of serious health problems.

The ants are good at **foraging**, or looking for food. Pest control workers now use new types of baits that make use of that fact. The baits have grains of poison that are like tiny breadcrumbs. The ants take the grains to their underground home, and they share the grains with other ants. In this way, the poison gets to a large number of ants.

bedbugs in the United States is an example. The chemical DDT was once used as a pesticide. It was very effective. When sprayed in a place, the chemical lasted a year or more, and it killed many types of bugs. Scientists found, however, that DDT could harm the health of animals and people. As a result, its use was made illegal in the United States for most purposes. With no DDT to stop them, pests like bedbugs began to come back.

The return of bedbugs may have been helped, say some experts, by increased travel. Though the bugs were nearly gone from the United States, they remained alive in large numbers in other parts of the world. It may be that the bugs were carried from abroad by travelers. More people are traveling than ever before.

23

Dogs can smell bedbugs even when humans can't see them.

"The thing that I like about pest control, I can sum up in one word," says pest controller Jim Rutherford. "It's a challenge." When Rutherford went into pest control, he was not expecting to enjoy it. But he soon realized how interesting it was. "At the end of the first year, I [realized that] every house is different. Every day is different," he says. "The insects don't change very much, but the houses do and the challenges do."

Another thing that changes is the field of pest control itself. Workers have to keep up with it all. In the past, they often used strong chemicals that were very good at killing pests. Today, some of these poisons are outlawed. Others

## So You Want to Be a Pest Control Worker

People who become pest control workers receive general training in the safe use of pesticides. They usually get this training from the company that hires them. They also need to have special **certification** from their state. Among the specialties in which they might get certification are general pest control, rodent control, termite control, and the method of killing pests with poisonous gas called **fumigation**. A typical training period for one certification is 10 classroom hours and 60 hours on the job. Long-time workers commonly have a number of certifications. After they get a certification, workers have to take more classes in order to keep it. By taking new classes from time to time, workers learn about changes and new approaches in pest control.

Most pest control jobs require at least a high school education. Many pest control workers have also attended college. People who want to work with larger animals can get animal management degrees. Students in these programs learn

about different pests. They study the ways that animals fit into a habitat. By knowing about the habits of pests, workers are better able to fight them. Students also learn ways to figure out about how many pests are on the scene.

Some people who study pest management find jobs in zoos and in research stations. Others go to work in wildlife centers. A number of government jobs involve pest control.

This worker is checking the poison bait in a rat trap.

can be used only in limited ways. Workers no longer just kill pests with poisons. They have to be more scientific in their approach.

## Science and Skills

"When I first started, in 1989, if I said I was a professional pest control worker, people didn't believe I was a professional," says Rutherford. The work keeps becoming more scientific, however. He predicts that at some time in the future, pest control workers will "need to have an **entomology** degree."

Entomology is the science of insects. It is key to many types of pest control. People who do well in pest control are good at natural sciences. They can see problems clearly. They understand the importance of planning. They like going to different places to do their work, instead of sitting at a desk.

### To the Dogs

Jack is one of a number of dogs that Jim Rutherford has trained. Rutherford first found Jack, a yellow Labrador retriever, at an animal shelter. The dog was about half a year old. Something drew them together, and Rutherford brought Jack home. People said that Jack caused trouble, but Rutherford figured that the dog was just misunderstood. He knew that Jack needed to run a lot. "So I gave him a job," he says.

Rutherford trained Jack to sniff out live bedbugs. He put live bugs in boxes and filled other boxes with other things. When Jack found the live bugs, the dog was rewarded.

Now Jack goes to work with Rutherford. A worker who looks for bedbugs can find them by sight only about 30 percent of the time. But a trained dog like Jack can sniff them out about 90 percent of the time.

Working in pest control involves plenty of contact with customers, too. So workers need to be good at talking to people and understanding people's feelings. Not only do workers go onto people's property, they deal with people who are in the middle of a problem. Their customers may be upset. They need help and advice.

Many workers start as helpers, or apprentices, in a pest control business. They get training both in classes and on the job. After getting experience, some workers start their own businesses.

Whether they work for themselves or for someone else, pest control workers

A pest control worker points out damage done by termites.

continue to take classes—both to keep their certification and to stay on top of new ideas and new methods. For example, one of the newer ways to get rid of bedbugs (and some other pests) is to heat a room with special heaters. The high heat kills the bedbugs and their eggs. The heating has to be done very carefully to avoid starting a fire or causing damage. Things that can be harmed by heat, such as plants, have to be removed from the room.

27

## Happy at Work

Rutherford has taken his own business to a new level. He trains dogs to find bugs. The dogs help workers make sure that all the pests at a job site are eliminated. His dogs are in demand around the country.

The dogs are part of a trend. Because pesticide chemicals can be dangerous, people are looking for other ways to fight pests. Methods considered "green" are being used more and more. Such methods cause little or no harm to the environment. "Our industry has really made a shift toward turning green," says Rutherford.

Green workers often use natural materials, such as dirt that comes from certain kinds of **algae**. Algae are living things similar to plants. When some types die and then rot,

### Going Green

Green methods of pest control fit in well with an approach used by many workers in recent years. This approach is called Integrated Pest Management (IPM). IPM is a way to fight pests with more than pesticides. It relies on many different methods. It tries to use poisons as little as possible. In this way it aims to cut down on the pesticide poisons that show up in food or harm the environment.

With this approach, crop growers use less poison. They rely instead on planting methods that help prevent pests. Also, they try to drive pests away in ways that don't use poisonous chemicals. They try to use traps when they can. In cases where they need to kill pests, they may still use chemicals. But they try to use the ones that are least dangerous. Where possible, they may use other ways of killing pests. For instance, they may make use of natural **predators**—animals that naturally feed on the pests. The predators are brought in by the pest control team to do the job.

A scientist shows equipment used to test for dangerous chemicals such as pesticides in the water people drink.

their remains turn into a substance that can cause bugs to dry out and die.

Finding new pest control methods is important for the future. Rutherford says that anyone interested in nature, science, the building trades, environmental protection, or health care could enjoy this line of work. "I wake up seven days a week pretty much happy," he says.

29

# GLOSSARY

**abatement:** A reduction in something—for instance, an action that makes a problem less serious than it was.

**alga:** A certain kind of living thing that grows in water or in wet places. It is like a plant in some ways but lacks roots, stems, and leaves. The plural of alga is algae.

**allergy:** A condition in which a person feels ill when he or she comes into contact with a certain substance.

**bait:** Something such as food that can attract a pest. It might also contain poison or might be used to catch the pest in a trap.

**certification:** A record showing that someone has passed a test or knows about a certain subject.

**creature:** An animal, often a scary one. Scary imaginary things that act like living things are also often called creatures.

**entomology:** The branch of science that studies insects.

**foraging:** Looking for food.

**fumigation:** The use of a poisonous gas to kill pests in a room or building.

**habitat:** The place where an animal or plant normally lives.

**microchip:** A tiny electronic device made of a material such as silicon.

**pesticide:** A chemical used to kill pests. Chemicals used to control pests in other ways—such as by driving them away—are also often called pesticides.

**pheromone:** A substance given off by an animal that gets a response from other animals of the same type.

**predator:** An animal that hunts and eats other animals.

**professional:** A person who has expert knowledge of something and is paid for using his or her know-how.

**respirator:** A masklike breathing device that can protect against dust and poison in the air.

**virus:** A tiny life-form that lives inside larger living things, often causing a disease.

## BOOKS

Brown, Jordan. *Micro Mania: A Really Close-Up Look at Bacteria, Bedbugs & the Zillions of Other Gross Little Creatures That Live In, On, & All Around You!* Morganville, NJ: Imagine Publishing, 2009.

Collard, Sneed B., III. *Science Warriors: The Battle against Invasive Species.* Boston: Houghton Mifflin, 2008.

Gussoni, Clizia. *The Awesome Book of Bugs.* Philadelphia: Running Press Kids, 2008.

Markle, Sandra. *Termites: Hardworking Insect Families.* Minneapolis, MN: Lerner, 2007.

## WEBSITES

**http://www.bulwarkpestcontrol.com/pest-common-to-your-area. php?page=learning-center**
The Bulwark Exterminating company's website offers an online library of information about pests, along with pictures.

**http://npic.orst.edu/pest.htm**
This website of the National Pesticide Information Center includes fact sheets on pests and pesticides, along with links to additional useful websites in nearly every state.

**http://www.pctonline.com**
This website of the magazine *Pest Control Technology* has the latest in pest control news.

**http://www.pestworld.org**
This is the official website of the National Pest Management Association.

**http://www.pestworldforkids.org/index.html**
Also from the National Pest Management Association, this website has games, guides, and science fair kits for kids.

**http://www.sfgate.com/columns/askthebugman/archive**
This page of the *San Francisco Chronicle*'s website provides links to articles about pests and pesticides written by "The Bugman."

**About the Author** Jessica Cohn is a writer and editor with an extensive background in educational publishing. She has written numerous reading and reference books about careers, aimed at both students and adults. In her own career, she has been called upon to write pieces as varied as textbook materials and the sayings on grocery bags. She lives in Westchester County, New York.